A Just Right Book

Thomas's ABC Book

Based on *The Railway Series*
by the Rev. W. Awdry

Photographs by Kenny McArthur, David Mitton,
and Terry Permane for Britt Allcroft's production
of *Thomas the Tank Engine and Friends*

Random House ⌂ New York

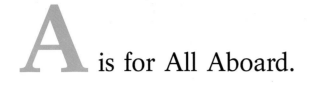 is for All Aboard.

"All aboard!" says Thomas the Tank Engine.

B is for Bertie the Bus.

Bertie is Thomas's friend. Beep! Beep!

C is for Coaches.

Annie and Clarabel are Thomas's coaches.

D is for Diesel.

Doesn't Diesel look grumpy today?

E is for Edward.

Edward, a kind engine, helps everyone.

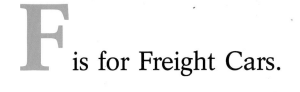

F is for Freight Cars.

"Trick-trock!" say the silly Freight Cars.

G is for Gordon.

Gordon is a big, strong engine. Poop! Poop!

H is for Henry.

Here comes Henry under the bridge.

I is for Important.   **J** is for James.

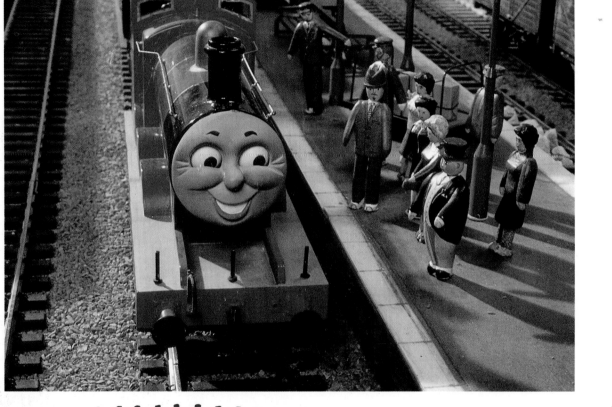

James is going on an important journey.

K is for Kind.　**L** is for Little.

Kind little Edward is careful with freight cars.
Wheeesh!

M is for Men.

The men who drive the engine stand inside the cab.

N is for New.   O is for Old-fashioned.

Toby the Tram Engine is old-fashioned, but he has a nice new coat of paint.

P is for Percy.

Percy is a little green engine. Peep! Peep!

Q is for Quick.

James the Red Engine comes to a quick stop.

R is for Railroad.   **S** is for Sir Topham Hatt.

Sir Topham Hatt runs the railroad.

T is for Terence the Tractor.

Terence likes to talk to Thomas.

U is for Up. V is for Valley.

Here comes Thomas up the hill.
See the valley below.

W is for Whoosh. **X** is for eXpress.

Whoosh! Gordon the Big Engine pulls the express.

Y is for Yard. Z is for Zip.

Zip! Zip! Thomas is busy in the yard—pushing and pulling. Isn't he a Really Useful Engine?

DARWIN